The Seven Ages of Man: From Shakespeare's "As You Like It" ; Illustrated

William Shakespeare

Transfer from Circ. Dept.

* NCF

THE

SEVEN AGES OF MAN.

FROM

SHAKESPEARE'S "AS YOU LIKE IT."

ILLUSTRATED.

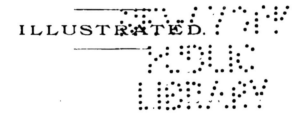

PHILADELPHIA:

J. B. LIPPINCOTT & CO.

LONDON: 15 RUSSELL ST., COVENT GARDEN.

1885.

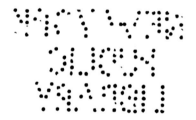

J. B. LIPPINCOTT & CO.

LIST OF ILLUSTRATIONS.

All the world's a stage,
And all the men and women merely players:
They have their exits and their entrances;
And one man in his time plays many parts,
His acts being seven ages. At first the infant,
Mewling and puking in the nurse's arms.
And then the whining school-boy, with his satchel
And shining morning face, creeping like snail
Unwillingly to school. And then the lover,
Sighing like furnace, with a woful ballad
Made to his mistress' eyebrow. Then a soldier,
Full of strange oaths and bearded like the pard,
Jealous in honor, sudden and quick in quarrel,
Seeking the bubble reputation
Even in the cannon's mouth. And then the justice,
In fair round belly with good capon lined,
With eyes severe and beard of formal cut,
Full of wise saws and modern instances;
And so he plays his part. The sixth age shifts
Into the lean and slippered pantaloon,
With spectacles on nose and pouch on side,
His youthful hose, well saved, a world too wide
For his shrunk shank; and his big manly voice,
Turning again toward childish treble, pipes
And whistles in his sound. Last scene of all,
That ends this strange eventful history.
Is second childishness and mere oblivion,
Sans teeth, sans eyes, sans taste, sans every thing.

All the world's a stage,
And all the men and women merely players:
They have their exits and their entrances;
And one man in his time plays many parts,
His acts being seven ages. At first the infant,
Mewling and puking in the nurse's arms.

And then the whining school-boy, with his satchel
And shining morning face, creeping like snail
Unwillingly to school.

And then the lover,
Sighing like furnace, with a woful ballad
Made to his mistress' eyebrow.

Then a soldier,

Full of strange oaths and bearded like the pard,

Jealous in honor, sudden and quick in quarrel,

Seeking the bubble reputation

Even in the cannon's mouth.

And. then the justice,
In fair round belly with good capon lined,
With eyes severe and beard of formal cut,
Full of wise saws and modern instances;
And so he plays his part.

The sixth age shifts

Into the lean and slippered pantaloon,

With spectacles on nose and pouch on side,

His youthful hose, well saved, a world too wide

For his shrunk shank; and his big manly voice,

Turning again toward childish treble, pipes

And whistles in his sound.

Last scene of all,
That ends this strange eventful history,
Is second childishness and mere oblivion,
Sans teeth, sans eyes, sans taste, sans every thing.

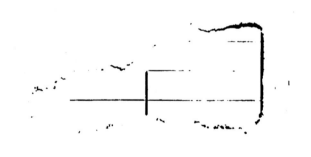

Lightning Source UK Ltd.
Milton Keynes UK
21 March 2011
169614UK00003B/8/P